IN THE BLUE HOUR

Praise of
Carrie Magness Radna's Work

In the Blue Hour, the new collection by Carrie Radna, carries the reader across borders (Italy, Egypt, 5th Avenue and 59th Street, NYC), and through musics (Mozart, Brahms, "Rhinestone Cowboy"), into the heart of a speaker engaged in what might be called meditations on blue. Like William Gass's *On Being Blue,* and Kate Braverman's *Squandering the Blue, In the Blue Hour* dissects numerous kinds of blue—the blue hour, the Blue Grotto, blue Chevrolet, and many kinds of blues—holiday blues, pocket-size blues, typewriter blues. Its lessons can be painful. In "I wear his sadness like a shirt," the speaker learns that "Loss does not feel like cotton." But they can be exhilarating, too. "Can we repair the sky?" the poet asks, and answers yes, once we get above the clouds. We live in a world where Buddhas appear alongside monuments to Trump. *In the Blue Hour* looks hard at that world, sometimes close enough to spit, sometimes far enough away to soar. It's a good, blue ride.

–Tim Tomlinson, author of *This Is Not Happening to You,* (stories), *Requiem for the Tree Fort I Set on Fire,* (poems) and Co-founder, New York Writers Workshop

Carrie Magness Radna is a poet of light and shadow, time and space, inner and outer oceans. Every hour holds years of meaning, and those meanings contain the seeds of their opposites, as a disaster contains all the beauty in the universe: "After lightning struck / the weeping willow, / I saw all the tiny flame-bits / that showered the bark whole / resembling stars ... I, covered in ash, was cleansed." She invites us to walk a path that turns and shifts with the progress of sunlight through trees; sometimes we get turned around, hypnotized by the changing light, but always we are led home by the stars that have grown inside our skin. Always, we know how lucky we are to be alive, to be light: "Floating on a makeshift raft, / but not alone, not dying yet."

–Sharon Mesmer, Poet, professor of creative writing at New York University and the New School

In the Blue Hour is a collection of poems about love "stripped raw" but with "honey-sap inside". Carrie Magness Radna's voice is both tender and tough as she explores her attachments to a sometimes cruel world, and her poetic techniques are deftly displayed at every emotional pitch. I recommend especially "Purple Things" and "Lily" for their exploration of melancholy, "Music Is an Anodyne" and "Melted Rain" for their trenchant and wistful evocations of passing time, "Dilated at Dark" and "Sarabande" for their depiction of the touch that separates or unites — but all of the verses, whether on music, place (local and world-wide), memory or love, are vibrant and alive.

–Robert Scotto, author of *Moondog* (winner of 2008 ARSC Award for Best Research, The Independent Publisher Book Awards 2008 Bronze Medal for Biography, an entry in the 2nd edition of The Grove Dictionary of American Music and is the basis of an upcoming 2020 documentary), and poetry collections *Journey through India and Nepal* (2010) and *Imagined Secrets* (2019).

Carrie Magness Radna's *In the Blue Hour* is a fine book of poetry, which at times sounds like the blues, especially when it sings of the city dwellers, the lines unrushed and precise:
"Streets are now bluer. The windows, colored either in butter or goldenrod, are bleeding their light as mist from architectural honeycombs; The lights from street level explode like hot magma—cars speed on, double time . . ."
It is a book of memory– of parents, lovers, men, women, damaged or lost; of sadness and pleasure, of loneliness and struggle with depression; of a chaotic world on the brink of destruction; a book of longing:

"Man, woman, and those singularly defined,
we cross the paths to the future primed
without a road map, without explanation,
we exist, moving from station to station"

–Anna Halberstadt, author of *Vilnius Diary* and *Green in a Landscape with Ashes*; translator of *Nocturnal Fire* and *Selected Selected* (in Russian)

In the Blue Hour is introspective, observant, feminist and playful. This visual book of poetry paints pictures, like the artists Carrie Magness Radna references throughout, and shies away from nothing: depression, love, loss, love lost, male toxicity, sexuality, and even hangovers. These poems are playful and have sass; one poem imagines sex with Peter Gabriel and in another, she writes, "I don't date monsters." And, in another she skillfully writes, "Fold me like a burrito in a canoe." Many of these poems explore something so important, something I wish I read more poems about – depression. But even when these poems are their bluest, they still have hope. They still have humor. They still surprise. This is a wonderful book of poetry that explores the complexity of what it means to be human.

–Chrys Tobey, author of *A Woman is a Woman is a Woman is a Woman*

Beauty, love, and melancholy are Carrie Magness Radna's themes. Her soft and gentle voice is elegiac. At their best, her poems present memorable images and metaphors that transcend our tragic limits. She might be called Keatsian in that her best poems convince readers that truth and beauty are one "and all [we] know and need to know." For example, 'In the sky,' a love poem spoken to her partner in the morning, imagines the need to restore the beauty of the blown lights of the heavens. As it starts to move to its conclusion, Radna describes glories of the natural world and the flight of herself and her lover:

I woke up in the morning fog, sweet and fragrant berry-green;
.... loose invisible, silver threads were hidden in the queue

In the sky vast and unending like love should be, ...

Below the sky we could fly in our minds
And repair the cracks no one else could see.

Impressed by the paradox that the imaginatively true is not the truth of reality a reader might think of the lines of Juan Ramon Jiminez translated by James Wright:

... how lovely, how lovely
Truth even if it is not real, how lovely.

–Mike Graves, author of *A Prayer for the Less VIOLENT Offenders: The Selected Poems of Mike Graves*

In this collection of poems, Carrie Magness Radna slowly turns a kaleidoscope of muted colors offering a palette that changes from bright orange skies to grey moon nights revealing a view of her life and her world as a work in progress. Her stories span the full range of human tragedy and foibles but the heart of the book lies in her personal story. The colors of her story are varying shades of blue that capture a lingering melancholia as she examines her life choices and their consequences. She paints a penetrating portrait of a life in question and the pursuit of honest answers. A fascinating glimpse at the inner workings of a creative mind's process of self-discovery and revelation through poetry. A powerful and illuminating read.

– Phillip Giambri, Author, *Confessions of a Repeat Offender* and *The Amorous Adventures of Blondie and Boho*

Blue infuses the firmament from which many of these poems descend, depend, impend, often clouding, precipitate with actual rain and sometime snow (inevitably melting), inundates "an inner ocean", others real -- lakes and rivers -- that "flow like water" below. It varies widely, from the

paint on "fantastic" cars ("big and fast as spaceships") the poet dreamed as a child, to the blues playing "loudly" in her head, coloring mood to "rare indigo," to true. "I swim in (or I am) an imaginary sea," she writes (in "Keep breathing"), "crashing against the rocky street." This is a voice not heard in the wilderness but a cry emanating from a metropolis. Very soft, very clear, it breaks on the ears and enters the mind in a curious amalgam of city racket combined with waves one can see and feel and enter as though the soul were bare feet. There's an emphatic cadence to these poems, one that begins as it ends, suspended on the page, sometimes where it lands, sometimes reaching outwards. Poised alternately between the ascension of art and immersion in quotidian waters, between refinement and candid observation, forthright, associative, and free, with interpolated trills of operatic tremolo, covert confessional notes caught between chronicle and reflection, *In the Blue Hour* archives recollection's collage.
–**Jack Cooper**, editor/co-publisher, *Poets Wear Prada,* and creator of These Are Aphorithms https://aphorithms.blogspot.com

If I were to assign a color to the spectrum of Carrie Magness Radna's *In the Blue Hour*, it would not only be blue, but purple, to signify the poet's passion, the royal color that she opines has many layers, *like fresh blood oozing from dark roses and violets.* Ms. Radna gives nature and human nature such a lyrical, musical, and radiant twist, posing melodious and imaginative philosophical questions (*Can we repair the sky?*) from poem to poem that etch indelibly like delicate pieces of art. In this gem of a collection, both melancholy and beauty coincide with the blooming of flowers and the endless sky, and the reader willingly follows as Radna takes us on her real and metaphorical travels. With a child's exuberance and an adult's acuity, she turns family secrets, dark clouds, and muddled hearts into pearls of wisdom and a rebirth of joy (with a few well-aimed digs at Donald Trump, to boot). These poems will fill you with hope and song, and even within the blueness, they will comfort you.
–**Cindy Hochman**, editor-in-chief of *First Literary Review-East*

IN THE BLUE HOUR

American poet **Carrie Magness Radna** is an archival audiovisual cataloger at the New York Public Library, a singer, a lyricist-songwriter and a poet who loves to travel. Her poems have previously appeared in *The Oracular Tree, Tuck Magazine, Riverside Poets Anthology, Muddy River Poetry Review, Mediterranean Poetry, Poetry Super Highway, Jerry Jazz Musician, Cajun Mutt Press, Word Doodles Lit Mag, Brownstone Poets Anthology, Home Planet News, Walt's Corner, Polarity eMagazine, The Poetic Bond (VIII-X), Alien Buddha Press, Rye Whiskey Review, First Literary Review-East, PoetsUnplugged.com* (podcast), *Jersey Poets Plus!* (podcast), *Songs of Selah, Shot Glass Journal* (Muse-Pie Press), *Poet's Corner, Nomad's Choir, BigCityLit* and *The spirit, it travels: an anthology of transcendent poetry* (Cosmographia).

She has published two chapbooks, *Conversations with dead composers at Carnegie Hall* (Flutter Press, 2019) and *Remembering you as I go walking* (Boxwood Star Press: self-published, 2019) and her first collection *Hurricanes never apologize* (Luchador Press, 2019). She won third prize for "The tunnel" (category: Words on the Wall: All-Genre Prompt) at the 69th annual Philadelphia Writers' Conference (2017). She also won 12th place for "Lily (no. 48 of Women's names sensual series)" by the 2018 *Writer's Digest* Poetry Awards. She recently won an Honorable Mention Award for "all trains are haunted" in the 89th annual *Writer's Digest* Writer's Competition (Non-rhyming Poetry).

Born in Norman, Oklahoma, she is a member of the Greater New York Music Library Association (GNYMLA), and is a member/have read/workshopped for the New York Poetry Forum, Parkside Poets, Riverside Poets, Brownstone Poets and Nomad's Choir. When she's not performing classical choral works with Riverside Choral Society or New Year's Eve performances with the New York Festival Singers, or writing art song lyrics with her choir buddies, or traveling, she lives with her husband Rudolf in Manhattan.

IN THE BLUE HOUR

POEMS

CARRIE MAGNESS RADNA

Nirala

Nirala Publications
4637/20, Third Floor, 310, Hari Sadan,
Ansari Road, Daryaganj,
New Delhi 110 002
www.niralapublications.com
niralabooks@yahoo.co.in

First Edition 2021

ISBN 978-81-939367-6-4

Cover Design : Tarun Saxena/Graphical House

Cover Photo: Carrie Magness Radna

Author Photo: Carrie Magness Radna

Printed at
Print Ads Press
New Delhi-110092

Preface

In 2017, I was mired in many shades of the blues: a life-changing trip to Italy, my husband's firing from his job, and a bout of anxiety and depression which lasted for an entire year.

Between these events, I attended the 69th annual Philadelphia Writer's Conference (PWC), as per suggestion by my fellow NYC poet Katherine Hogan, who needed a roommate. So I went, and my life was transformed in 4 days.

At PWC, I attended two poetry workshops, headed by Yolanda Wisher, then the Poet Laureate of Philadelphia (Master Class: Mood Indigo) and Portland, Oregon's own Chrys Tobey (Turn toward me: Social Commentary in Poetry).

Their classes began a burst of active creativity, which lasted for two years, when I wrote many blue poems and political poems. Many of them made it into I*n the Blue Hour*, and some of them were in my first poetry collection, *Hurricanes never apologize* (Luchador Press) in 2019.

Also, during the conference I befriended the fabulous and talented members of The Mad Poets of Philadelphia, who thought I was fabulous too.

At the end of the PWC, I was the 3rd-place winner (category: Words on the wall: All-Genre Prompt) for my poem "The tunnel." That lit the fire – and eventually I got some my poems published!

A poet was officially born.

Blue is not just a color. It's a state of mind, from sublime to devastation. A call to nature (the sky, the ocean, flowers, etc.) and the city. A humbling mark on holy objects. A genre of art/music. And my favorite time of day: Before the night comes, when the golden light and the pink of the sky fade into beautiful blue.

Even in these blue times, we are not alone.
#Alonetogether

Stay safe and well.

– Carrie Magness Radna
July 2020

Contents

Part Two
INNER OCEAN

To Rudolf

My blue-eyed funny valentine,
my true blue love

I love you forever

IN THE BLUE HOUR

POEMS

Part One

Can we repair the sky?

In the sky

If all the lights blew out, can we repair the sky?
Fastening the odd velvet to the outer atmosphere,
with tacks shaped like stars,
it was all ours like a hair breath, like a lone church bell chime.

But all alone, I did sew up the bits of invisible clouds with silver thread.
and as I rested my head upon your chest for a short rest,
while the horizon began to bleed orange and red,

I woke up in the morning fog, sweet and fragrant berry-green;
the sheen of the twisted, black-barked tree blocked the perfect view

of me and you kissed by the sun,
loose, invisible silver threads were hidden in the queue.

In the sky, vast and unending like love should be,
trees growing strong in the green, above the bluest seas,

below the sky, we could fly in our minds,
and repair the cracks no one else could see.

The Tunnel

Everyone else follows the light, but I'm more interested
in how sound travels within; will my song
vibrate the walls with a great intensity,
or will my dulcet tones and notes of a nonsensical scat---

Da da, da da dum, di di dum

be buried within the walls as the traffic racing in the Lincoln Tunnel
towards New York fly past?

Will my voice ride at the end of the tunnel, joining the light?
Will anyone hear me eventually?

Studded Buddhas

She missed the Q32 bus.
Her attention easily distracted
by two white, baby Buddhas at the window next to Trump Parc.

Studded with green and blue horns, they are tiny devils
wearing mirrored and glittered Chanel and Gucci bomber jackets.

Fashion is the new religious order,
especially when on Fifth Avenue.

Trump Parc is abandoned by the new High Order;
it will soon become a new Pret à Manger.

She spits at it as she passes,
her heart choosing not to be corrupted,
but she still missed her bus by one whole minute
at its stop across the street on 59th and Madison.

Even when no good deeds go unpunished,
the bad choices will catch up and run every one of us down.

Beautiful fog

A grown tree, more stump than branches,
alien to the Northeast with lesions growing
out of the ground, like fat tumors catching against a hillside,
but still trying to bear fruit after 10 years in the city---
I feel like this sometimes.

Today my melancholy mood has painted
something beautiful; even in the fog,
the leaves are brightly colored, while birds are constantly leaving.

The rings of my life are present at last, my tears a welcome baptism,
as I relay all of my fears to those I love.
The bark has been stripped raw; nothing but honey-sap inside.

And as I unburdened myself,
I felt blooms sprout out from every lesion,
those troublesome tumors I have carried,
my fears that they were cancer,
and the true words unfolded the new petals, one by one
into gorgeous bright pink blooms where no sickness or blood
runs into.

I always thought my melancholy was a sickness
I needed to hide from the world, as if it was cancer,
but it painted a watercolor picture of my inner landscape,
as Monet did for his beloved water lilies.

This touch of malaise is not deadly, after the unburdening;
maybe the constant exhaustion will eventually stop
when love blooms more true and fruitful.

After the long family discussion,
when the inner notes ring true again,
when the sentiments are fully baked in the best-made bagels,
when the water dripping from the beautiful fog outside
nourishes the tree of your life,

hugs are again delicious,
and he holds your hand close all the way home,
where you sleep for a while deep and soundly,
before the opera begins tonight, before the work is finished,
before the balm for your psyche is found
by the talking cures; they help create healing
rivers for the tree to stand upon.

Purple things

(No. 5 of E verses)

The dark matter is strong in me today.
It doesn't always mean that I'm depressed.
Like the color purple, once worn by royals, is often now considered the territory of females and effeminate males; these shades can carry many, many layers, like fresh blood oozing from dark roses and violets when they burst forth and decorate the fertile ground, their mistresses are caretaking the blooms; these lovely blooms prefer the light of the twilight and the dawn, unbroken by the horizon.

I would walk many miles to reach you, my dear.
You have inked your shoulder
once again with tangled ivy and purple flowers, in remembrance of your departed sister, but the sweet cat hiding its face in the blooms is for me.

I may not decorate my skin,
but your name is already tattooed on my heart
the first time I saw your face; when I see purple things, my heart jumps gladly, and the dark matter I carry around sometimes, many happy stars are born instantly in it during our exchanges.

Lady of the Lake

Before intermission, I kept staring at Jean-Yves Tribaudet's great hands
as he played notes of Schumann, his *Scenes from childhood*
and his first piano sonata without any sense of melancholy.

Melancholy was my mistress while growing up,
she was constant; not only an odd flavor of my personality,
but she stayed back in the wings for the longest time, until tonight.

After intermission, I felt humiliated;
these past 24 hours I already felt on edge,
but then melancholy stepped up to the mike,
kissed my consciousness,
and presented my prize: a bag of shame tears.

As the lovely Tribaudet played Ravel's *Miroirs*
like an effervescent and revolutionary read of a Frenchman's
bedtime story,

I pictured all my tears grew into a lake outside Versailles,
and like the Lady of the Lake,
(without carrying Excalibur or snaring a future king)
from Kit Williams's *Masquerade*.
I swim laps in my lake
for hours without stopping.

Lily

(No. 48 of Women's names sensual series)

Her bullet-stung lips stayed dry,
a brand-new Cupid's bow fashioned by silicone;
her eyes, red and puffed up from a good cry,
she lacquered on her mascara as she silently moaned---

upon the E train, where no one truly cares
about any stranger's case of hidden heartache,
unless, when budding poets ride along, they would dare
to witness in her shallow gaze, each secret earthquake

she's carried in her head all day. Without even speaking
she told her tales of woe, the ethereal spin
of her silky, raven hair hanging free, unwashed, but seeking
any known solace of the pounding of her chinny-chin chin

where gravity will gain its influence again, claiming its karmic reward
(perhaps in one or two years from now), when
her Cupid's bow finally flattens into its normal shape,
loosening its guard
against any intruder who'd want to stick it in---

she stares deadly on, as if she were already tricked,
winning a half-won life she had never dreamed up
for herself, where the good ones would stick
around to fill her magical cup,

making her life easier, it was never meant to be;
now she's a sad, painted doll riding solo on the E---

I will be his muse

I will be his muse;
he is already mine.

But, unlike all the rest,
I will not hold my sweet tongue
and won't go with the status quo

And as the birds continuously sing,
the water grows deeper at the lake
we one day will reside and make

And the traces of the banks are
sometimes washed away
without regret or remorse

And so my love, one day will be ours
as the young people disappear from the crowd

We will return to the water
where we will wash up our bones
and our children our stories and music
only the birds could ever sing.

Capri sun

After we exited the Blue Grotto in thin rowboats,
the sun met us outside,
dissolving the inner indigo into outer golden light

(we were blinded for a whole minute, floating, bobbing, exposed
under a perfect sunlit sky, us wiggling like fish)

Out on the main yacht, we bathed under the sun for almost an hour,
us women wearing bandeaus and bikinis,
before the sea called to us to dive into its cold,
cold blue waves dotted with light.

Blue Nile

Too far from Egypt, I made it to Capri
in one day a year ago
and I remain spellbound---
the color of the Mediterranean Sea
intoxicated me, so I dived into it
without holding my breath.

As the lonely Moors
came upon the mystic, azure water,
we laid back in the tour boat
to peer inside the The Blue Grotto.

It's another wonder of the world like the Nile,
with a different vibrancy and buoyancy.
We were all made luminous;
no one felt blue on that day.

It was the last perfect day
before the knife fell down,
before marauders stole our pure joy,
before the storm rolled in,
hitting the water in a perfect blue hue.

Afternoon tonic

(African streets in Florence)

If a tonic could be made
from the afternoon
I got lost in Florence's streets,
discovering a hamlet
seeing children laughing on roofs,
Ethiopian fruit sellers arguing and
haggling in brightly colored clothes
and other Africans conversing in
French in outdoor cafes.
I got lost there, but I found
adventure and exuberance
for a while---

I want a drop of that afternoon
to cool me down when hot,
to warm me up when cold,
to stir up my gumption
when boredom sets in---

My happy hour Frappuccino
has chocolate and coffee in it,
with some caramel notes,
sweetening the afternoon.

This tonic helps me now
when the kids come in from school;
now I feel awake and alive again,
and I dream of Firenze,
its cobbled streets,
and its African people
setting the afternoon on fire.

Meditation at Heceta Head Beach, Oregon

Resting my eyes upon the Pacific,
crows gather in the crusty cliffs,
where lonely creeks lap water
from the shadows of the forest parks,
sparked by strong bridges and their supporting trees.

They merge finally with the sea, near Highway 101,
where the sea lions gather and come,
and children are born fearless
under the great winds from the mountains,
sheltered by emerald leaves and black-barked trees.

Cradled by multi-colored hardy sea grass,
the stones have no jagged edges to them,
no danger of cuts or jabs to tender bared feet,
slate-colored, they are too heavy to skip upon the waves.

Shaded in ancient algae, the rust-tinged waves tempered
by old azure; touching a baby boy sky
laced with confectioner's sugar clouds,
the creamy waves crash and crest harshly
as they have done for millions of years,
the obsidian rocky shore, full of moss and secret sounds
drowned out by the unceasing wind.

If my imagination materializes into a makeshift man

Hold on, girl, you'll never get away from me.
I have marked my territory around your camp with tracks of my blood
so the monsters and God's death call won't come knocking here,
and I'll mark up and down your body with my sweat and pheromones.

Oh babe, you love it when I bound you tight upon the bed.
When your breath fogs up my glasses, I swoon inside,
but I try to keep my vulnerability hidden, because I'm the dominator
(Go ahead, darling, surrender to me!).

And when I whisper words inside your ready ear,
you must write them down, so I can live forever,
(And don't even think of burning
my demands into ash while I'm gone!)

I know that you love and crave my touch;
no matter what the other folks say, I'll make you holler
and scream (and come) in both pleasure and pain.
(Do you love it? I know you do…
Even when folks call you crazy
because of your big ideas, well, thank you).

So hold on, girl, (wait your turn, dammit!) you will never get
away from me.

Chimera of Arezzo

A chimera: my ex
was both a snake and
a fire-breathing lion,
hiding his two faces well.

His dashing Tuscan good looks
snared me at first glance; his pidgin English
sounded so sexy in his Sienese accent,
and he loved to collect art
made in the Etruscan Age.

But jerks don't stay hidden for long.
His anger boiled over constantly
when his ragu was a-salted,
and whenever the neighboring wine selections
tasted like random vinegars.

"All your cuisine is as good as Amtrak pizza,"
he would often taunt.
"All Americans must be stupid---"

I ignored it at first,
but then I counterattacked
with my dizzying intellect,
which was my Pegasus—

He found a shadowy companion;
and he screwed her brains out,
so we were soon done.
I don't date monsters.

Thoughts during a Viking funeral

(No. 4 from E verses)

As I watched sparks ignite the surface of the lake
outside of our house along with the budding sun,

I remember him, in every bit and breath,
in each thought and deed, all that we did together---

I stared sadly at my hands, as the boat with his body
burned cleanly and silently in the water;

before I said goodbye to him, my beloved lover and friend,
I wondered aloud: "How did my hands become old woman hands?
And, who will keep them warm from the cold?"

This was his last wish, to dissolve in opposing fire and water elements,
to be as one with nature at last, without leaving his bones lying
and wasting away in the ground.

This is not the time to swim towards him.
I still have work left in this world to do,
but now my tears fall, blending with the edge of the lake---
I wish my shouts would also extinguish the ship's fire.

I wear his sadness like a shirt

Hours before when I heard the news
of the passing of an old friend of my friend,
I want to keep him company; I wear his sadness like a shirt

His smiles and jokes he wears outside I see with his chosen family,
until we are alone in empty hallways,
I feel his profound loss through his soft gaze
I wear his sadness like a shirt

No time for brewing tea,
the moving men are here to carry the rest of the room's contents away,
the walls are white and empty, his shirt is black and cotton;
I wear his sadness like a shirt

Loss does not feel like cotton,
more like heavy wool one's skin can't breathe in,
and we both breathed in so easy as we held each other;
I wear his sadness like a shirt

I wish he could feel my love
(it would make him breathe easy like cotton).
Leaving him was so hard to do,
especially since he left his loss with me

Right now at 2 am, I let my own emotions take center stage,
tears fell down my nose, my heart beating hard in my chest.
I wish I didn't have to leave him; I wear his sadness like a shirt

Keep breathing

I will keep breathing even when caught in the dregs,
near the old things gathering dust that are safe from the rain,
and the remaining ruminants who chew their cud silently,
they all commute on the morning rush train for many miles.

The smiles of the haggard causes me alarm
when he instructs when and where to step down
and take out my umbrella;
the gingered-haired girls dyed their hair green, remembering Spring,
rain falls down like in Spring, but now it's Fall---

And the cold cold cold is beginning to blow forth, unrelenting.
Notes not made for most humans now hum in my brain.
I know what I'm doing and who I am, but for a while
I swim in (or I am) an imaginary sea, crashing against the rocky street.

Piano trio

It'll probably be the last time we'll get to sit on these red velvet seats, so enjoy the spell as we sit a spell---when the spirits of the old music hall infect our heads, staring out at us with marbled eyeballs rolled back, cock-eyed when the head wound's oozing, gazing, waiting---nodding to the beat of the music.

We sat up in rapt attention, watching the cellist dance with his bow and strumming fingers; his best friend, the pianist, made colors with his fat and fast digits, digitizing in emotion; the violinist, young and sharp as a lance, followed both Masters' timbre and time carefully, though we could hear the hidden genius budding; he will be a legend in 10-years-time.

The piano trio was written when its composer was still young; one can see the bones, the steps towards genius status, circling as the ghosts come to rest, hovering over the red velvet chairs, smiling at the sound of it.

Music is an anodyne

Before the hot tears,
before isolation and jealousy,
Mozart's music
transformed innocent air molecules
into imagined butterflies
(some beat their rapid wings on my clavicle)
and all the ghosts of the great concert hall cooed and sighed,
and we saw the stars again
before tonight's rain.

As a harp

Inspired by Henry Cowell's short piano pieces and NYC Pride Parade

We could all play our pianos by stroking its insides
as if the strings were part of a harp,
almost pushing the velvet-bottomed pedals away with our fingers
(so the piano is never prepared…)

I heard restless female spirits screaming; the water lapping
against the rocky shore,
rainbows forming in the sky I can't reach yet.

I couldn't reach anything; even him, who needs the most sunshine
and the happiest of the populace who are visiting the city for the first time,
kissing openly in the streets, never damned like fallen angels

As memories glide away, the piano-harp sounds its call,
coloring true, modulating from a short alarm to a soft coo:
How I missed you yesterday, my beloved friend,
while you were busy enjoying the parade, or, were you?

Sarabande: Autumn sweater

Words by Carrie Magness Radna (c2017) ; music by Mark Fiedler (c2019)

This city always keeps me awake.
Alone in this hotel bed, taking long, deep breaths,
I try to memorize the exact color of your eyes.

The sweater you packed for me is for autumn, not for winter.
With a slight shiver, I recall that radiant time you wore it,
how warm your arms in mine, how the bare skin of your neck,
as I tried to kiss it, smelt like mead.

That was years ago and you've grown cold;
too cold the air, and dark now to go wandering.
How many more nights to miss your enfolding arms?

I can tell where the stars are, even in this faraway city.
I pray to keep warm enough to get by.

My heart is a hunter (Reset)

Twilight was falling
so I ran after you
towards a house alone in the moors,
I wonder which one of the lights is yours

My heart is a hunter,
and with it I carve out a horse
so I can get closer,
and the fever in my soul
makes me run like a stallion

Do you know why I want you so?

Beyond the trees
my spirit is flying
and I feel I'll never get back down
without crying
but you bring me down to earth
as if I was a phantom

With one simple touch,
I reset my brain,
and as my feet land
back on the ground,
peace floods in

That's why I want you so much

You are my touchstone
and when you are away,
I'm nothing more than
a whisper in the wind

I want you back here today;
that is why my heart is a hunter

Marrying into mental illness

Little by little
he had diminished her light
with his darkness

Sacrificing every
unborn pseudo child
into deep seas,
they all regenerated into
new life forms,
crawling towards land

Only the aged could understand
the sick and deluded souls
who try to rise above
any other form of madness

She wanted to stay safe,
so she married him,
but he was lying to her
about himself at the time

In the night forests, tigers roam free,
filling their victims with their hollowing
which only they could hear;
they see the tree falling down
even though it makes no sound—

And the things beloved from childhood
are still measured and tolerated,
giving the affected some peace
in a crazy world

But toys need to be put away
when one comes of age,
she was taught this lesson early;
he never learned it

Instead of having a child,
she takes of him as if he's a child,
him embracing an arrested development
of his inner being.

She had waited for years,
staying too long at the fair
for her man to show up
to save her, instead,
she wears the knight's armor,
tossing horseshoes to win
a few moments of peace
without him.

Winter Solstice 2017

I.

Scandinavians are not the only worshippers of Yule.
Tonight will be glorious, even in Sweden, where darkness
is constantly constant like the heaviest of black wool veils,
where ceremonial candles are finally lit with happy chanting.

Evergreens are brought inside to protect the home with ancient magic,
from the cold, brutal winter until Spring.
The Yule log is burned in the fireplace, in remembrance of Celtic sacrifices,
for another kind of protective magic.

Now Europeans drink wassail and stare at the fire,
silently making wishes for the upcoming year as they play cards,
waiting for all the candles to burn out.

II.

Yesterday I picked up two forgotten, cut Christmas tree branches
from the street.
I took them in, and smelled the evergreens deeply before mounting them
upon a framed portrait by my front door.
I hope the Yule/Evergreen magic would protect us now.

III.

Anxiety is the demon of the season, and it has struck me down hard,
unrelenting, without gentleness or joy.
My chest feels as it's been jumped upon by a tiny, invisible baby kangaroo,
(between embryotic and grown kid stages),
my head is filled with swirling dust.

My place has been crying out for attention, it's been weighed down and ill.
I've been ill, slowly covered in dust,
my love's bubble of denial has finally burst,
he sees the crap carnage, and has sprung to action.

IV.

The face of the red Persian rug in my foyer is finally uncovered,
we haven't seen it in an entire year.
Wendy the home organizer is coming this weekend
to help send and store the junk and unneeded items away;
the 3-day weekend contains Christmas, so we can
clean and sort on the free day, the holiest day of the year.

In the darkest and longest of nights, it is holy;
the light will break through as the junk
of the last year is cleared away---

Blue

My father's mother had beautifully shaped legs;
blue and numerous varicose veins
shot out of her pale skin, resembling a fine Stilton cheese.

Her words, once upon a time, left marks
upon her loved ones' souls---
her bitterness often poisoned the room.

Now she has lost some teeth in her senility.
She can now finally eat
without knowing her sons' names.

Her bitterness came from the blueness of her youth;
she passed down the blueness to my father, and to me.

I look down at my own feet, and I see
new blue veins protruding from the skin,
but my heart is not bitter.

I am true blue, compassionate like my father
and my mother, who both had blotted
the old bitter things from their vocabulary.

Blue Chevrolet

Rhinestone Cowboy blared loudly
on the dashboard 8-track,
as we kids were dropped off at school;
Daddy didn't care for Disco much.

Long lines for gasoline
grew long every day for many months.
American-made cars were hit the hardest,
especially Fords and Chevrolets.

Daddy drove an Impala in the '70s.
He favored those painted in both red and maroon shades.

I rode in the back seat,
dreaming of fantastic blue cars,
big and fast as space ships.

I wished that someday I would hold
my special someone close in one of them,
on the blue vinyl seat
like lovers do in the movies.

Opening up

It was just a green lacquered trunk bolted at the end of the bed.
Nana is now dead, and her harsh admonitions of never breaking
the seals were now silenced. We took our time opening up the
space: the windows, the random dresser drawers, ourselves....
We poured some wine, leaving some water rings behind. Finally
the trunk was opened. Oh, what treasures we had found!
Nana's and Papa's marriage license from June 1945, each passport
from each decade, each water-stained, teary letter they had sent
to each other during the war. Baby photos, fat-cheeked
girls and guys from the Fifties, my mom's face (which now
my niece wears on her own face), beaming softly
as she smiled shyly, wearing a white graduation gown.
Mom now sat by me, her face now lined, still beaming.

Holiday blues

I want to be a bear, to growl a lot and wear
some fur, and fuzzy socks with foxes' heads on them,
and I want to curl in bed, sleeping deeply until Spring.

Long nights are a-coming to get me,
the long dress rehearsals for holiday musical merriments,
the after-dinner mints are out-of-bounds for the singer's throat now,
just hot tea, honey and the occasional self-slap across the face to
stay awake.

Words come out in spurts, as I try to capture and hold them still
for long enough, so I can do my work; my head still spins,
and the blues play loud in my head, coloring my mood to a rare indigo,
during these times of sheer madness
when peace and love should be the only thing of importance.

Blues, pocket-sized

Hear them scream
out lyrics that cream their jeans,
leaving the girls wet as they dance

Music's a favored drug for kids
and elders alike; sometimes you see them
standing together at the same venue,
grooving along to the beats

Heating up each known sense, common sense
is done for; another pocket-sized novel
in poem form is set to a catchy tune,
as the guitars lay it down

And the lady's singing is never fat;
she'll sing all night if she wants
under a blue spotlight, as her followers
try to get closer, still as the groans

from the Roland mimic steel guitars,
that's groovy for sure, in any cadence
that the folks can possibly follow

In the bluest hour

In the bluest hour,
I wait for you to come home
even when you are there
I still feel alone
and sometimes you'll stare
in your look
where love used to lie
now it's like seeing back
two black holes in the sky

I stole the last line from a song
I stole the last line from a song,
when it's true, it's not wrong

In the bluest hour
I remember long-ago April showers
that fell down so hard
when I made love
with my first lovers

You said I was your first
even in the worst of times
when great sex hanged out
lazily on the line
with you it never really rained
we were too dry

When I recall
those bluebells that grew
out on the Texan highway
pointing towards home

where my family still stays
it's been years since I've been home

But you won't roam
You said: "Why can't you stay home?"

I have to see the world
to find some hidden happiness
but I guess
you don't want to come with me

In the bluest hour
I gain some power
but only by myself
when I'm most like myself
is not with you
is not with you
I regain some blue

America, June 11, 2017 and May 14, 2018

My take on Allen Ginsberg's poem, "America"

6/11/17

America, dump Trump. Stop being such pansies. I can't wait to get my rainbow tattoo (guess every one of us is a little gay).

America, you are not your own special planet: buy you, for you, with you; I'll play with you, but I also want to play with the entire world.

America, tell all my sisters they can do anything at all; I'm still waiting for the extra 27 cents so we can all be equal.

America, insure us once again, never mind most of us are poor and brilliant or even poor and stupid, or marginalized into whatever categories you plan to place us.

America, are we still free?

America, are we too brave, or scared to say anything at all?

America, I changed my accent when I moved to the Northeast. Your depiction of my native drawl, which I keep under lock and key until I reach OK and TX is maddening. You make us sound like stupid hicks, like saucer-eyed infants, like highly aerobic deer-caught-in-the-headlights from your stigmatic scrutiny. Please, stop it y'all.

America, you know far too much about me already--- Facebook's got its meat-hooks in me, sometimes the meat is rotting; everyone now knows about my recent trip to Italy, that I still silently support the now absent Hillary, and which olive oil I use ---wait, I thought that was a secret. Dammit!

5/14/18:

America, the ladies are now speaking up, and they (we) are pissed. The old boys' club is becoming a thing of the past, the old sexual harassments and assaults are now in the spotlight, and the boys are now paying up, resigning from established posts of industry and are ushering in their new disgrace.

America, why can't we stop the violence? (In schools, nightclubs, movie theaters, sporting arenas, churches, synagogues, even trucks slamming people in the streets. Why aren't we stopping the selling of guns to young and/or crazed individuals?)

America, are we still a nation of dreamers? Why do we have to send the Dreamers back to countries they never knew, since their parents tried to find both solace and work here?

America, a Californian biracial woman, who's a divorced actress, a humanitarian and spokesperson for women's and human's rights, is marrying into the British monarchy this week. This will be a good thing. Meghan Markle is not Wallis Simpson (a Nazi-loving, oversexed, unpleasant cow). We should pay attention.

America, when will we ever learn when to speak and when to shut up?

America, is fake news real news, is real news really real, or is it fake as well, and how will we tell the difference?

America, are we still free? (Maybe...)

Is this now America

Thanks to the latest news,
my heart is flattened like a National flag,
folded over and over again,
its stars are still showing;

(don't want to touch the ground,
don't want to be burned,
I want to fly free and high,
but it's never the right time)

Children are still separated from their parents (for profits),
their families just want a taste of freedom,
away from their insurmountable hardships.

Mr. President,
why are you making their lives harder?
When will they be reunited,
when the background checks
and important forms have been filed?

Is this now America,
whitewashing immigrants?
Is this now America,
not owning up to our foibles and mistakes?

My heart is like a flag;
I want it to spread it out
and inspire everyone I see
oh say can you see

Thanks to those in charge,
our little lives are beginning
(not) to count,

(and with these stripes we are healed)
and we do feel the pain
while the marks remain invisible,
invincible.

Part Two

Inner Ocean

Pathos

At the end of the life of each ancient Greek, they only asked one
question: "Did he have passion?"
Pathos, the word for passion, is now roughly translated as sorrow.

Many wars and shifts in reasoning may have dulled or shifted the seasoning
of the first original Eros, separated from erotica, enthusiasm,
even simmering the odd ducks, who crave to sit upon the great
thinkers' laps,
reading their words loud to a captive audience.

But accents are often changed to get ahead, books hidden, family
names Anglicized,
works authored by those only known by their initials,
holy writings favored over romances,
family duties lie waiting.

People love the wrong ones;
passion becomes sorrow.

My love is covered in a gaffer's tape of pathos,
shifting between one extreme to the other,
caught in mid-suspension, barely breathing.

My passion, I keep it hidden
when the sorrows come creeping,
finally letting it out of its cage
in the tender moments before sleeping.

Johanna, the fishmonger's daughter

(No. 23 of Women's names sensual series)

Trouble only courts those
who don't accept life is long.
My sister's got her mind made up,
she'll leave the shore on her own.

Since I left the red list,
I'm not dangerous anymore.
My fresh flesh, like our fish,
you can taste it at the store.

And all the fishermen
call me out from their boats,
"Johanna, yo, JoJo,
when you're heading to shore?"

I can't help that I'm a bit delicious,
I'm not shaped for the farm.
My skin tastes like salt water,
just a little won't do you harm.

While my lips are burned by the sun,
I'll wait 'till you kiss me hard,
then I'll rub some Chapstick on
and keep your kiss on my mouth
until I'm sailing south,
towards home.

And all the fishermen
call me out from their boats,
"Johanna, yo, JoJo,
when you're heading to shore?"

The sea is full of good things
as far as our eyes could ever see,
If they do ever dry up,
where would we, as a race, would be?

Through I've been hung out on the line
it's never for long.
I catch more than I can keep
and I toss out more than I can hold

Sometimes men resemble fish,
sometimes fish resemble men...

And all the fishermen
call out from their boats,
"Johanna, yo, JoJo,
when you're heading to shore?"

I still want to stay out
in the water
a little more.

Indigo statue (in the Future)

Inspired by Jay Chollick's poem "Blue"

To Jay Chollick (1928-2020), a brilliant artist and poet,
and a true friend and teacher to all of us. RIP

When my baby says goodbye
to the big, awful, blue world
by his hand or not,
paint my organs in blue
like the nudes of Matisse,
as I wear black
for the rest of the year;
my heart beats blue
with its sinews and veins
so both love and obligations
won't be in vain—
the whole damn year of mourning
will be blanked out
with the blessed sun,
my lungs and skin will hold
the same melancholic tincture
until
eventually the sun
will shine for me again,
changing my body and visage
green in its golden light,
then, normal again
as if the tragedy never happened,
never frozen in place—

when my baby is gone
if my baby is gone.

Dream no. 901 (Peter Gabriel)

In my warm bed,
I was having sex
with an angel
named Gabriel

His wings were not soft;
his skin was.

Or, did I stup
Peter Gabriel of Genesis,
circa 1973,
while he was in his
cult music getup

he would wear a flower head on stage, his face white with black-lined eyes. Was he ever an angel?

His older self,
bald in a black turtleneck,
worldly, powerful,
sans wings and white makeup

tucked me in bed tight
so
I could sleep soundly

without
shocking the monkey
with a
sledgehammer

Twilight at the upstate shack

Wonder what is on the living room television
at this hour of the day
when the blue hour takes hold
of the house, transforming
it into a magical spot
ready for nighttime?

Mom is still driving on Route 71;
5 minutes away, she's bringing home
roasted chicken for dinner; her family
is bored, sunburned
from a day at the pond.

Daddy is airing out his sandy shoes
out on the porch; he pours some wine
and sets out some Italian salami
he knows his wife likes,
with some aged Parmesan

and the kids are still bored
in front of the TV
as night grows deeper.

Orange

You never liked the color orange,
even those mod hooded sweatshirts the cool kids converge upon—

The sky is now colored orange.
Long days without regrets is what we can ever strive to,

but fear could be called orange
by most people. You hated to show any fear; your closed heart

could had been colored orange.
Once I thought you could cure my loneliness, like Vitamin C.

See, I can't rhyme with orange!
What a cruel joke for all poets, seeing sunshine with only one eye

open, while cutting wedges out of oranges,
lemons and limes, trying to dress up another drink for Happy Hour.

Melted rain

Yesterday's snow was short;
it fell fast and quick, disappearing
off apartment buildings and scaffolding
as rain, melting, hitting the heads of passersby
the morning after, in a bright day of sun,
making accidental mini-rainbows
dancing in sewage grates.

Sickness done, I must breathe easy.
Back to work, I join the crowd again
as we drive through underpasses and bridges
where the new melted rain
flows down easily.

Inner ocean

(No. 49 of E verses)

I do want to go outside today,
but my inner ocean volcano
has erupted; waves are crashing
into consciousness
and I hold my breath in sharply

floating effortlessly
confuses my whole being;
where am I supposed to go?

Fold me like a burrito in a canoe
so I won't repel and cause
any known stress
when I reach shore

the red time's coming soon
the rain will start up again tomorrow
but I cannot move
until I can hear the water move no longer.

Man pool

Surrounded by massive levels of
testosterone at the bar,
I'm swimming in a titillating
hellish man pool;

I need some ladies to break up
this Kevin-laced swamp,
their ironic wives are allowed in.

Some of my friends
would call this Heaven.

I gasp and grasp at straws,
hoping I don't dissolve
into the mist—

My appetite for this energy
is unsated; I strike and stroke
for a seat in the girl zone.

But after my plate is clean,
I will escape,
trying to get clean
from this toxicity.

The men discuss court terms,
stupid edits and smokin' hot women
with shaved vaginas.

I try to hover towards the surface;
I wish I can swim like a fish—

Morning twilight

Stockholm to Vaxholm, June 1994

Hangovers strike deep in the land of the midnight sun.
The sun never actually sets there in midsummer;
there remains a perpetual twilight lasting a few months---
O, sleepers, awake!

The bars close at 3 am; a sliver of silver sky
points to the nearest McDonalds
(their burgers are not completely beef;
I have no beef about it; we need to sober up)

And this dude didn't kiss me, one of my cousin's friends.
Why didn't he kiss me? Why didn't I kiss him?
Why am I such a chicken-shit, even while traveling?
---Yah, who needs him?

As the car sped on the road back to Vaxholm,
I saw a pond heavy with misty clouds
as if it existed on another world;
the sun shone at 4 am; it wore a 9 am cloak lined with river-
grass.

So far away from home, I was happy with a throbbing head.

The bowl

If one lives in a bowl
made of two mountains:
Bitterroot and Sapphire,
then the weather is always mild:
the snow will fall slowly
upon the gathered leaves,
but in the summertime,
when the fires come,
the air is constantly filled with smoke,
even on the clearest of days—
one dreams of once gazing
tenderly at the stars above,
but we need to follow the river,
one hour south to Lake Como,
where happiness begins
on a lazy Friday,
but still attached
to the original bowl.

Pickle

(c. 2005)

Her summer bag caught my eye;
pickle-green encrusted with rhinestones
as I devoured hot French fries
on 42nd St. between 9th and 10thAvenue.

Sometimes I wonder how she came here
from point A to B, giggling as her
pink tank top hugged her deep curves.
"She's a knockout," I thought. So young

and full of promise. So am I, still. I smiled as my eyes
focused on my love, pulling apart his
open turkey sandwich with a Swiss Army knife. He's one
of the reasons I've lingered in New York, also a new career

far away from the prairies. A gay couple argues about
living room furniture as I stare at my man, sipping my
Cherry Coke. Life is no longer a pickle, or even
a solid color washed away in the rain.

Knife in wood

I just had to let it go,
like a fat blade from a Swiss Army knife carving
into a gnarly piece of living wood.

To let what go? I ask myself.
My youth, creativity, bravery or gumption,
so I can keep him safe from becoming unglued again a fourth time
or I have kept myself too reeled inside,
so that all the blood remains inside my skin
so I can keep warm without a fire?

Sometimes I am not happy,
but luckily my biggest inner voice
is a future version of me,
who is more fulfilled and content than present me,
whose music still moves me in many, many ways,
rivaling the best sex I've ever had.

I am counting the days
until I see my parents again (in a week)
until I finally travel on EuroRail (maybe in a few years) and
until I am finally happy with the concept
of not having children of my own (maybe I'll get there after
menopause).

But my song is still strong, I communicate fairly well,
and my love for my dear ones is beyond infinite.
I still have many things to say,
and the Universe is the greatest teacher.

My muse is a dirty bird,
but my conscience remains a Girl Scout,
trying to stick it to the dirty bird most days
with the blasted mental knife…

But I just had to let it go,
like a fat blade from a Swiss Army knife aiming
into a gnarly piece of living wood.

Sea-change

The top of an ancient Jewish temple now graces the ceiling
of the LGBTQ temple in West Chelsea, as art.

The old roof is now formatted in my mind
as a makeshift watercraft, completely watertight—

I sail upon it in the wild, untamed ocean, looking for her.

My third eye is a deep pool;
not to suffer fools gladly there.

My husband may be a fool; I barely suffer through his jokes.
He has a good heart, forever faithful.

Even when the rain washes away the anger,
the fools are laid to rest under my careful gaze.

I should remain dry, attached,
but the inner-sea shouts a change;
the dream-times flow like water,
full of beautiful women.

Marmalade

Lately my fantasies have grown feminine,
stroking women's skin naked, while kissing
ruby-lacquered lips.

This is just a reaction to a referendum on sex with my current love,
or … is it?

And, when she appears in my dreams, riding along on a makeshift raft
on the great river; her face touched by sunspots and freckles,
her hair a fuzzy marmalade shade, with blue eyes laughing

I know that this vision, and she, must be just a recurring dream...
or, is it something else, coming soon, out of the horizon
as I softly drift in and out of consciousness

I shake in bed, sweating
for many nights
as my man lay sleeping?

Shadows and light

I can see other faces when I watch TV;
they seem so real, as if they were my friends.
No, they are images, and I'm alone
since you've been gone---

And the shadows grow thicker
inside the house; the flicker
of the screen light acts as a beacon,
between hopelessness and cocooning.

This can't be real.
The loneliness is palpable;
its greedy touch keeps me up at night---
I miss the graceful light of morning;
now its harsh glow mocks me.

The glow of the screen is comforting
in the darkest of nights. It's my link
to the world. The real world has forsaken me.

Why did you have to go?
What did I do to you?

Did you have to sell your soul
to the shadows—did you lose
rights to the light
after loosening the unholy knot?

Or,
you just don't care
about me anymore?

Hard candy

He always wanted love
more delicious than
hard candy

couldn't ever get enough—
never could quench down the fire
in his loins, in his mouth

and she was red-hot
once upon a time,
before their kid, before the fat

settled in—circus peanuts
made the palette bland
before the big top show,

but he still wanted spectacle,
the sexy girls melting like chocolate
and cherries, popping.

But his heart gave out
before he lost her, he lost it all;
life no longer sweet,

ravenous, tastes now dulled,
moving slower, sugar dripping
into water; basically breathing,

melting into nothing,
spun fine; staining mouths pink,
thinking he's young again.

Sonnet of 2 deaths (no. 40 of E verses)

Within one singular breath
is the distance between life and death,
for ones not yet born and those who have been here,
young, old, straight, queer--

Man, woman, and those singularly defined,
we cross the paths to the future primed
without a road map, without explanation,
we exist, moving from station to station

sometimes armed with knowledge, sometimes learning nothing--
Life is sparked, lit and burning true, then snuffed out, a done thing.
Did we wonder what we would have done if we knew,
if this were the last time? Suspicions grew

fast, and blame and grief, and guilt too, they last; the memories overpower
all the consolations of well-wishers, the inner never-ceasing shower
from utter loss, feeling like rubbish, without hope or certainty.
What is life now without my loved one beside me?

Our baby had checked out early; what can we do now?
The snow falls fast upon the farmer's plow,
even after tragedy, we keep on moving; one must not wait,
so others can be fed, and to not suffer the same fate.

For all are invited to Death's door,
let's pray it's not our time to go yet, remain here a little more.

Rivulets of anger

Anger mostly breathes fire,
but her anger slowly destroys
stone as water,
cutting into ancient
mountains of resentment,
with hot and cold rivulets over time—

She kept her chin up,
smiling through the pain;
her lover caused her heart to swim
in troubled waters.
The rains fell hard as her
resentment grew strength
year after year—

Until,
until,
until

The rocks gave way—
breaking from a newly-formed water fountain
when her will was finally broken:

Her anger became sorrow;
her love is now dead,
the one who had twisted her heart
and left it to dog paddle in the lake.

The rivulets of anger did their job
beautifully—her stone sanity
churned into watery carnage and chaos
for a while,
finally freeing the all-consuming tension.

Steady

(no. 10 of E verses)

Steady as it comes,
this big love is becoming too much

Like a bull
it rushes in, fast as lightning,
slamming me against the wall

I have nothing against you;
I hope you are also
in this, in-the-thick too…

It's been so long, but does it
sound like me, being the steady one?

Why should I always be the steady,
the straight-man when I'm with you?
Do you know the things I can possibly do?

Please don't twist my words around;
just because sometimes I need to be alone,
doesn't mean I don't love you anymore…

If you are currently following the score,
the bull doesn't always win,
but then, I'm not always the matador.

I'll play along with this familiar song…
both of us can…do…

Why should I always be the steady,
the straight-man when I'm with you?

Do you know the things I can possibly do?

Eyes

At lunch, you noticed my eyes for the first time.
As you described them: warm,
glowing, a ginger-brown cat seeking her shelter
from the noonday sun in the high sand dunes.

I noticed yours too: many greens, ranging from the tender blades of
grass where I rested my head
when I was young, the jade warriors of China
and their strong swords blazing,
and the sea of green, and its silver curling waves crashing---

They glimmer when you gain some insight,
solve a problem, delight, wonder, or gaze
longingly at my face across the table at lunch,
when you said my eyes were beautiful.

Yours are beautiful too, but I was breaking;
as your waves crashed upon my sand dunes, I gasped for breath.

River of Love

You showed me the path
towards the river
in the heart of the forest,
but you never told me
about the fire
and its destructive tendencies.

After lightning struck
the weeping willow,
I saw all the tiny flame-bits
that showered the bark whole
resembling stars,
and my constant sadness
that once tried to swallow me whole,
had vaporized for several blissful moments,

I, covered in ash, was cleansed.

I could have dived in deep
in the River of Love,
and would have swim through it, forever
until my heart stops beating
where thousands of thousands of men and women
would kill to spend time in it,
to drown in love.

The skylight is full of crystalized carbon,
where both sea and space pirates
secretly crave to spend
all their time in.

But please, God, leave me the river,
the beating heart of the forest,

where I can find and spend my time
with my love; its edges
surrounded by holy trees
alive with fruit,
that we may feed upon,
until lightning strikes us again,
vaporizing us into immortal bliss
as our bones wash away
into the river.

Adam

You could devour me right now.
My forehead must taste delicious from all the sweat.

I need to rest a bit on the bed;
you move like a whirling dervish most days.

I will my eyes to close,
but they refuse to
since you are still here.

Don't worry, Dear.
My boots won't leave a mark
upon your new raw mattress...

I confess,
I didn't always feel
so safe and comfortable here,
or in the garden.

The first time was madness—
Her kid dozed 10 feet away
from her raw bed
as she tried to dive in.

(Right now, this is a mostly harmless interlude,
especially since you made your timely joke
about certain bodily fluids leaving its traces over there...)

So allergic to apples:
How is this possible, my dear?

Ah yes!—
you could devour me right now.

Strawberry

I could feel his kiss in the back of my throat,
even when his lips stayed shut,
and after he left, I still felt the heat
from them on my own mouth

The last time my lips tasted greatness
was when I devoured fresh fragola in Venice
in a farmer's market by the canals.

It was in May, on a warm day like this one—

The sweet red berry
was as big as a baby's fist;
It tasted like honeyed sunshine.

Tonight's gelato was full of strawberry
organically grown from Italy.
It reminded me of Venice.

But it didn't break the spell
of tonight's kiss,
even when some gelato
lingered for a few seconds on my lips,
it melted instantly.

Typewriter blues

From the New York Poetry Festival, written on a Sterling

Untouched version, transcribed:

inuunpre n ouncingg G erman, I hold a steady gladdss
of cold brew, istweat and stew, waiting for you
and I still don,8t have a lot to say ab out a l of this
and still a l the keys stick on this Sterling
<
my moter8s favorite ty ewritter, w ich she had interited
and yet wit tis f actenating creature
I try to sato y u but sti

my fingers get in the way

Word-friendly version (what I meant to say):

Often in unpronouncing German,
I hold a steady glass of cold brew,
I sweat and stew,
waiting for you

and I don't have a lot to stay
about all of this...
and still all the keys stick on a Sterling—

my mother's favorite typewriter,
which she inherited,
and yet with this fascinating creature,
I try to say to you but still
my fingers get in the way.

Setting to water

Based on Episode 6 of BBC's "Years and Years"

In the future, as we become able to set
our dying memories into water bubbles as the rest of the world burned,
what will we remember, so that future generations
would record, debate on and take note?

Our dreams of sexy mermaids
as our partners lay sleeping beside us?
Our scrapes, escapes, attempted rapes---
the bad times as well as the good times?

I dream of water constantly
as the temperature continues to rise.
Floating on a makeshift raft,
but not alone, not dying yet.

Quiet hours

Without the everlasting touch of the Universe,
stars grow quietly inside the deepest bark of the skin—

Each day dies with a whimper,
another cool trick by Night,
she strikes the sunlight
with a dash of ill-resentment.

Star-bits travel towards the eyes:
Sandmen bewitch the would-be sleepers in their tracks, to sleep,
all lay down like dead trees.

But death is a long way off for most;
the quiet hours effects all differently,
mixing most memories and dreams into star-clumps
either ignored or enlightened
by the careful, touched, and sweetest dreamers.

Odd trance

Sky-blue bands of curved light
converge and emerge
effortlessly as music plays,
but I am the only one who hears it,

seeing a piece of the Great Beyond
before my years run out on a timer,
the hollows locked within the sunset
show me the way back,
but at what cost? I am different now,

floating around in imitational space,
where one still breathes and do not freeze,
before I'm jerked back into this world,
where kids still hold a grudge against the system,
wanting to maim others before they die—-

And lesser and greater losses are riding against each other;
those gaining are slipping out of reach, hiding within the cracks,
waiting to be found, before the dogs would sniff you out,
so you disappeared again
under bands of light.

Dilated at dark

Streets are now bluer. The windows, colored
either in butter or goldenrod, are bleeding
their light as mist from architectural honeycombs;

the lights from street level explode
like hot magma—cars speed on, double time,
shooting stars made by Toyota, Ford or Cadillac

as the stoplights pulse angrily. Stop! Go! Go away!
The sharply drawn lines are now blurred,
rain like, on the driest night. I can't see right

through my dilated eyes. The exploded lights
blinded me; I couldn't move—until
I felt his hand, leading me home.

all trains are haunted

good-natured buttered-up angels who tripped out from Heaven's Bar
caught their glittery shoes and minds between whirlwinds and dead turnstiles
they ride the empty trains constantly, getting out of the cold rain
night's gig at Washington Heights, perhaps a shade of its grandfather
took Sir Duke and Billy Strayhorn aboard towards Harlem in 1940
it's still midnight, almost the end of the line for randy trains—
it's now time to cruise over to Queens Plaza Yards, to sleep with warmed-up cars,
to romance that special one it met on the tracks at Hoyt-Schermerhorn
when they were hitched up for only a week—it never forgets
how it shined and smelled (no hobos slept in it)
its chrome face made the other trains shiver on the tracks
as they raced upon the third rail,
sparks flew—we rode the 1930s Vintage Special Train to West 4th Street
—it was haunted,
sputtering diesel as it rolled on slowly from Herald Square;
the lights went out three times
and a man stood in the center aisle, wearing a fedora and a caramel-colored long coat
as the passengers held carved, cream-colored handles in the mint-colored interior—
all subway riders are haunted by events:
broken hearts, tough-working days, able-drunkenness, despair, boredom,
longing for home or excitement, in every time or age.

The blue hour

Night gives Day the slip;
wearing her blue slip,
the sky turns blue
after the deed is done:
the Sun disappears, leaving behind
a trail of lithium-causing light,
gold mixed with tangerine and pink,
as the Sun sinks away West/South once again—
Night gets to work,
but before putting on her black dress
specked with stars,
before making her date with Mr. Moon,
she stays in her blue slip,
watches the Sun's deconstruction,
drinks her Happy Hour drink
in her favorite chair, and relaxes
as the humans rush home from work.

Evenings: Interior

I miss evenings up close and personal:

buildings honeycombed with butter and goldenrod lights,
the soft blueness of outside
making pedestrians walk quicker and lighter,

with weird promises of letting go each crazy day.
Now we all stay in,
no matter what time it is.

Recently, every 7 pm
our city shouts and claps in appreciation
for all medical workers starting or finishing their shifts—

a good way to start the night!
Even though I don't see the moon
rising from my window,

or have never seen the stars winking in years,
the evening still exists,
cutting the day down with its bleeding sun

and we all promise to let go.

Why don't the affected sleep? (6 + 6 + 3 + 3 + 4)

(inspired by Ein Deutsches Requiem, Movement 6: Denn wir haben hie keine bleibende Statt, by Johannes Brahms)

Comes the night a total mystery,
all do sleep except the affected by their inner inferno,
rebel-rousers raise their homemade flags,
poets haunted by their lightning words, struck by stars,
musicians troubled by the howling notes of the wind,
and all the dogs bark back their discontents—

Why don't the affected sleep?
They know that a storm is coming,
but they are not prepared
for Death's fatal sting,
where or when it will come to claim them,
crossing over, passing the key

for the nearest distant dimension
the living could never see,
hammers sound like electric guitars

and as hearts beat in heavy throats,
letting wounds hum in cold pools,
the wounded regenerate in dulcet tones—

What will become of our old haunts,
the bones that we leave behind,
when our dust becomes grass,
when the morning sun cuts out the night?

Acknowledgements

THANK YOU, Katherine Hogan, Yolanda Wisher, Chrys Tobey and The Mad Poets!

This book would be nothing without you.

A lot of other big THANK YOUs to:

Yuyutsu Sharma, and the gang at Nirala Books including Suresh Verma for publishing *In the Blue Hour* and for helping to bring my visions to life.

The beautiful blurb writers: Jack Cooper, Phillip Giambri, Michael Graves, Anna Halberstadt, Cindy Hoffman, Sharon Mesmer, Robert Scotto, Chrys Tobey and Tim Tomlinson:

Your gorgeous words are a balm to my soul during these crazy times.

The awesome proofreaders and talented writers who've noticed typos: Patrick Hammer (all poems), John Migliore (inner pages), Michael Graves and Jack Cooper:

Your quick eyes, attention to detail and wit helped *In the Blue Hour* get into fighting shape. THANK YOU so much for your helpful suggestions!

My family: Mom, Dad, Devon, David, Lainey, D.J., Courtney, Asher, Canaan, Rudy, Rachel, Richard, Raffi, Kat, Rebeka, Dev, Julian, Jovita, Seeth and the dozens of cousins:
Your encouragement, patience and support mean the world to me. I love you all!

Some of the poems included in the book appeared in the following journals. Gratitude is expressed to the editors and publishers for their permission to publish them.

Afternoon tonic (African streets in Florence): *Mediterranean Poetry* (https://www.odyssey.pm/contributors/carrie-magness-radna-2/) (1st posted July 26, 2019)

all trains are haunted : *Poetry Super Highway* (Poet of the week: February 4-10, 2020) ; Honorable Mention Award (89th annual Writer's Digest Writer's Competition (Non-rhyming Poetry: 2020)

As a harp: *Parkside Poets Collective* (2019)

Blue ; Purple things (no. 5 of E verses): *Riverside Poetry Anthology,* vol. no. 20 (2020)

Blue Chevrolet; Lily (no. 48 of Women's names sensual series): *Parkside Poets Collective* (2018)

Capri sun and Strawberry: *Mediterranean Poetry* (https://www.odyssey.pm/?p=4125) (1st posted July 25, 2018)

Chimera of Arezzo: *Riverside Poets Anthology, vol. 18* (2018)

Dilated in dark: *Home Planet News, issue #8* (November 2020)

Dream no. 901 (Peter Gabriel): *The Oracular Tree* (January 2019); *Parkside Poets Collective* (2019)

Evenings: Interior: *Poetry Super Highway* (1st posted April 11, 2020); *Word Doodle Lit Mag* (1:1 Summer: July 2020)

Eyes: *Poet's Corner: Good News from Good Shepherd* (Good Shepherd The Episcopal Church in Fort Lee, Fort Lee, NJ: April 5, 2020)

Hard candy: *The Alien Buddha gets rejected!* (Alien Buddha Press: July 4, 2020); *Sensitive Skin* (online: 1st posted September 9, 2020)

Indigo statue (In the Future): *Jerry Jazz Musician* (A Collection of Jazz Poetry: Summer 2020 edition: 1st posted August 24, 2020)

Is this now America: *Tuck Magazine* (http://tuckmagazine.com/2018/07/06/poetry-1595/) (1st posted July 6, 2018); *Brownstone Poets Anthology* (2019)

I wear his sadness like a shirt: *Hurricanes never apologize* (Luchador Press: December 4, 2019)

I will be his muse: *Muddy River Poetry Review* (Fall 2020)

Keep breathing: *The Poetic Bond* X (Willowdown Books: 2020)

Knife in wood: *The Oracular Tree* (2014)

Lady of the Lake: *Conversations with dead composers at Carnegie Hall* (Flutter Press: January 19, 2019; now out-of-print)

Lily (no. 48 of Women's names sensual series): 12th place winner of 2018 Writer's Digest Poetry Awards (awarded in January 2019)

Man pool: part of an one act play "The workshop" by The Parkside Poets, held at Good Shepherd, Ft. Lee, NJ (January 2020)

Marrying into mental illness: *Muddy River Poetry Review* (Fall 2018)

Melted rain: *Vita Brevis Poetry Magazine* (1st posted May 30, 2019)

Music is an anodyne: *First Literary Review-East* (March 2019); *Conversations with dead composers at Carnegie Hall* (Flutter Press: January 19, 2019; now out-of-print)

Opening up: *Eternal Snow — A Worldwide Anthology of One Hundred Twenty-Five Poetic Intersections with Himalayan Poet Yuyutsu RD Sharma* (Nirala Publications)

Orange: *Shot Glass Journal* (Muse-Pie Press), issue 27 (January 2019) http://www.musepiepress.com/shotglass/carrie_magness_radna1.html

Pathos: *The Poetic Bond VIII* (Willowdown Books: 2018); *Hurricanes never apologize* (Luchador Press: December 4, 2019)

Piano trio: *Conversations with dead composers* (Flutter Press, published January 18, 2019; now out-of-print)

Purple things (no. 5 of E verses): *Riverside Poets Anthology* (2020)

Sarabande: Autumn Sweater: words by the author (© 2017), music by Mark Fiedler (© 2019)

Steady (no. 10 of E verses): *Muddy River Poetry Review* (Fall 2019)

The blue hour: *Jerry Jazz Musician* (A Collection of Jazz Poetry: Spring 2020 edition: 1st posted May 12, 2020)

The bowl: *First Literary Review-East* (January 2020)

The tunnel: Third-place winner (category: Words on the wall: All-Genre Prompt), at 69th annual Philadelphia Writers' Conference (2017)

The tunnel; America: June 11, 2017 and May 14, 2018; In the bluest hour: written during the PWC 2017

Twilight at the upstate shack: *Vita Brevis Poetry Magazine* (1st posted May 23, 2019) (https://vitabrevisliterature.com/poems/twilight-at-the-upstate-shack-poem-by-carrie-magness-radna/)

Why don't the affected sleep? (6 + 6 + 3 + 3 + 4) inspired by Brahms's *Ein Deutsches Requiem, Movement 6: Denn wir haben hie keine bleibende Statt: Walt's Corner* (*The Long-Islander*: published Thursday, February 13, 2020)

Winter Solstice 2017: *Hurricanes never apologize* (Luchador Press: December 4, 2019) ; *Alien Buddha presents: Fuksmas, Chanfukkah & other of the year Fukkadays* (Alien Buddha Press: November 22, 2019)

Nirala Series

A Series of Contemporary Writing

Kailash: Jewel of the Snows
Rajinder Arora
ISBN: 978-8193936719 Paperback 2021 pp 268
plus 68 color Demy

A Short History of Nepal
From Ancient to Modern Times
Shreeram Prasad Upadhyaya
ISBN 9-788182-500174 2021 PP 255

Mother's Hand: Selected Poems
A Bilingual English/Nepali Anthology
by **Jidi Majia**
Translated into Nepali by **Yuyutsu RD Sharma**
ISBN: 978-8182500174 Paperback pp 96 Demy

Dancing in Place: *New Poems*
S. Renay Sanders
ISBN ISBN 81-8250-048-6 2019 pp. 64 Paper Demy

Blue Fan Whirring: *Poems*
Mike Jurkovic
ISBN 978-8182500969 2019 pp. 160 Paper

The Second Buddha Walk:
Inspired by The Second Buddha ,
Master of Time Exhibit at Rubin Museum, New York
Yuyutsu Sharma
ISBN 978-8182500983 2019 pp. 52 Paper Demy

Imagined Secrets: *New Poems*
Robert Scotto
ISBN 978-81825000442019 pp. 79 Paper Demy

The Tin Man
David B. Austell
ISBN 9-788182-500792 2019 pp.320 Hard Demy

All Vows:
New & Selected Poems
David B. Axelrod
ISBN 978-8182500822 2016 pp 194

The Dhimals: Miraculous Migrants of Himal:
An Anthropological Study of a Nepalese Ethnic Group
Rishikeshab Raj Regmi
ISBN 9788182500082 2016 PP 294 Rs. 295

Path to Excellence:
A Memoir by India's Distinguished Academician
Pritam B. Sharma
ISBN : 81-8250-0907 2017 Hard Cover pp 358

Word Has It, Poems
Ruth Danon
ISBN 81-8250-097-4 2018 Paperback pp 85

Eternal Snow: *A Worldwide Anthology of One Hundred Twenty Five Poetic Intersections with Himalayan Poet Yuyutsu RD Sharma*
Edited by **David Austell & Kathleen D Gallagher**
ISBN : 81-8250-088-5 2017 Paperback pp 309

Cats, Love & Other Surprises
by **Otis Kidwell Burger**
Illustrations by Katherine Burger
ISBN : 978-8182500891 2017 Hardback pp 65 RS. 1495

Letters from a Sacred Mountain Place:
A Journey through the Nepal Himalayas –
Photographs and Text by **Diane Frank**
ISBN 81-8250-095-8 2018 Hard Cover pp 144

Making of The Indian Muse
Context and Perspectives in Indian Poetry in English
Edited by **Goutam Karmakar**
ISBN 978-8182500273 2019 pp 430

Ritual: The Magical Perspective
Efficacy an the Search for Inner Meaning
Luc Sala
ISBN 9-788182-500617 2014 Hard pp.832 Rs.1495

A Blizzard In My Bones: New York Poems
Yuyutsu RD Sharma
ISBN 81-8250-070-2 2016 pp.134 Paper

Inside the Shell of the Tortoise
Poems written in India and Nepal
A Spanish English Edition
Veronica Aranda
Translated by **Claudia Routon** with **Yuyutsu Sharma**
ISBN 9-788182-500686 2016 pp.56 Hard Rs.395

Your Kiss is a River
Poems of Love, Food and Life
Carolyn Wells
ISBN 9-788182-500532 2016 pp.56 Hard Rs 195

Space Cake, Amsterdam
& Other Poems from Europe and America
Yuyutsu RD Sharma
ISBN-81-8250-059-1 2014 Hard pp. 110

Milarepa's Bones, Helambu
33 New Poems
Yuyutsu RD Sharma
ISBN-81-8250-032-X 2012 Hard pp.64

Little Creek
& Other Poems
David Austell
ISBN 81-8250- 031-1 2011 Hard pp.200 Rs.495

The Mystery Over Lord Buddha's Roots
An Analysis of the Mystery of the Shakya Kingdom
Mitsuaki KOJIMA
ISBN 9-788182-500563 2014 Hard pp.165 Rs.495

TEN: The New Indian Poets
Selected and Edited by
Jayanta Mahapatra & Yuyutsu Sharma
ISBN 9-788182-500341 2012 pp.134 Hard

Dada Poetry
An Introduction
William Seaton
Foreword by **Timothy Shipe**
ISBN-9-788182-500358 2013 Hard pp.112 Rs. 395

Libraries, Information Centers &
Information Professionalism in Nepal
Madhusudan Karki
ISBN 9-788182-500372 2012 Hard pp.348 Rs. 895

The Yeti
Spirit of Himalayan Forest Shamans
Larry G. Peters
ISBN 9-788182-500525 2014 Hard pp.128 Rs. 350

Folk Tales of Sherpa and Yeti
Collected by **Shiva Dhakal**
Adapted by **Yuyutsu RD Sharma**
ISBN 9-788182-500624 2014 Paper pp.125 Rs. 350

Annapurnas & Stains of Blood
Life, Travel & Writing on a page of Snow
Yuyutsu RD Sharma
ISBN 9-788182-500129 2010 Hard pp.200 Rs. 495

Trance, Initiation & Psychotherapy in Nepalese Shamanism
Essays on Tamang and Tibetan Shamanism
Larry G. Peters
ISBN 9-788182-500532 2014 Paper pp.412 Rs. 995

Tamang Shamans
An Ethnopsychiatric Study of Ecstasy and Healing in Nepal
Larry G. Peters
ISBN 9-788182-500099 2007 Paper pp.179 Rs. 295

The Pokhara Valley
A Traveler's Guide
LB Thapa
ISBN 9-788182-500198 2010 Paper pp.202 Rs. 595

Ocean in a Drop
Yoga, Meditation and Life in the Himalayas
Swami Chandresh
ISBN 81-8250- 005-2 2006 Hard pp.348 Rs. 495

The Price of Heaven
Travel Stories from India and Nepal
Evald Flisar
Translated from Slovene by **the Author & Alan McConnell-Duff**
ISBN 81-8250- 020-6 2009 Paper pp.140 Rs. 195

Student Politics & Democracy in Nepal
Meena Ojha
ISBN 9-788182-500259 2010 Hard pp.411 Rs. 795